My Little Teenage Brain

Beatriz Bernardino Paschoini

BookLeaf Publishing

India | USA | UK

Presentation by *BookLeaf Publishing*

Web: www.bookleafpub.com

E-mail: info@bookleafpub.com

ISBN: 9789363313101

First edition 2024

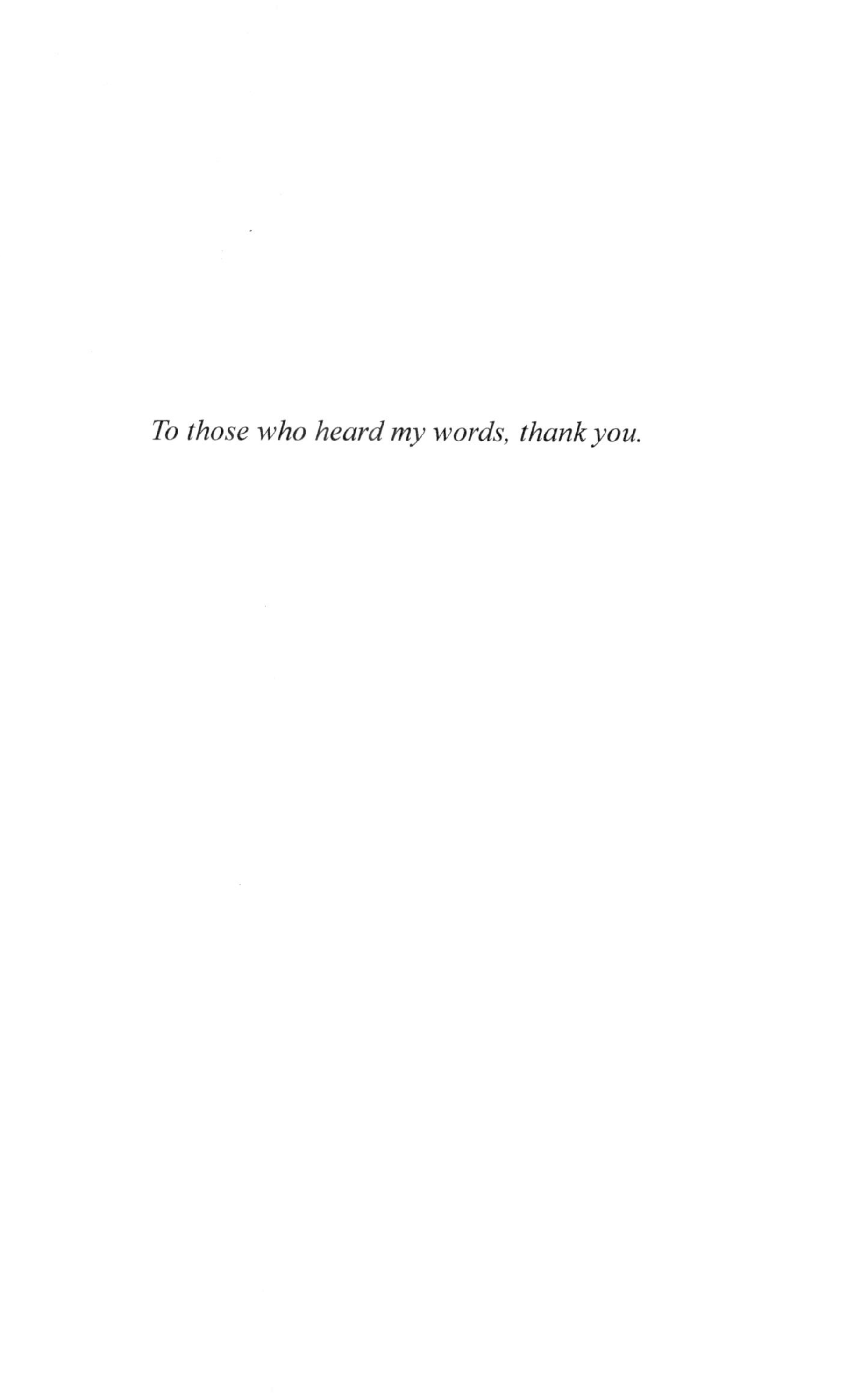

To those who heard my words, thank you.

ACKNOWLEDGEMENT

I owe my art to all those who showed me emotion: good, bad, and everything in between. I would not be who I am today without those who shaped me. I'm thankful to my first-grade teacher for guiding me in this great direction. For my best friends, for sticking with me through every terrible/questionable decision, which would later become art. For my parents, because I owe them my life in every possible way. For my siblings (blood or not), for teaching me how to be human, and for trusting me with their emotions. For those who loved me and for those who let me love them. And for so many more, for listening and believing in me.

future fallacies

The Future sits with me for tea,
He asks me how I'm doing and lays out some
plans.
In a fit of rage, I throw them into the sea,
I thought we were more than business, friends.

He calms me down and explains the mistake
made.
The Past sent a letter detailing my case,
All of a sudden, he starts to fade
And I find myself stuck in a maze.

As he fully vanishes, a note on the floor:
"Be wary of those you trust, for all is unwritten.
Don't hesitate to close the door,
Some things are better unforgiven."

I ponder what he truly meant,
What does he know that he keeps from me?
I wish for more guidance, someone to vent,
I put away the note and learn to be.

coffee time

I've never cared much for tea, so when I moved
to England,
I told all my friends that I'd "have coffee with
the Queen."
Now, 10-year-old me knew that dream was very
out of reach, and
I just wanted to brag about all the things I'd
come back having seen

So, we packed all of my dolls, all my best
clothes, and my favorite socks
I threw a pool party for all my elementary school
friends
I organized a little bag full of my prettiest rocks
And for the first time, I learned to tie loose ends

My crush at the time was this blond-haired boy
who I sat in front of
He wore glasses, and every time he looked at
me, we'd both giggle
4th-grade love isn't about much else, just laughs
and smiles, just to show off
And so our "relationship" had a bit of a wiggle

But I left for a year with no sort of
communication, and he was no more mine than I
was his
Over that year, I'd blushed for another blond boy
whom I never did kiss
I came back to find my past life shattered, and I
didn't even try to care
I was back home, where I knew it all, and
everyone I played pretend with was still there

I looked like me on the outside, and I felt like
me too
But my lips spoke English like I had a heavy
tongue
No matter how I looked for friends, I found only
two
Nonetheless, I felt all the good and loved being
young

After school every day, I'd go to the gym and
wait for pickup.
And we'd talk about all the things that had
happened
He liked her, she held his hand, it was a love
story with a beginning but no end
Simple feelings, new developments, and it was
our luck.

disclaimers

Deep down, I'm afraid my older friends see me as clingy
A somewhat crazy idea, I know
I really do like those who are younger than me, not just pity,
But I feel like I'm not enough of a good show.

Sometimes, I give my sister little breaks.
Spending a couple of hours apart, all it takes
For us to like each other and be ready to listen, no crime
But I wonder, what if she didn't have that time?

And whenever I'm bridging over the silence,
Because I feel like a roommate to a stranger
I hear a loud siren yelling danger
And I slow down for one second and pray for our alliance.

I don't need breaks from her; I have a heart that unconditionally loves
But I was born in a world where I wear "too much" as a disclaimer
Where I scream, but I think they all hear: "Tame her!"
And I wonder if I could ever love like she does.

like little me

I see myself in the way her long sleeves cover
her arms
How she walks with her head overthrown by a
cloud of depression
In the best of ways, I didn't need a succession
So I keep my eyes out; no need for alarms

She won't come to me, but that doesn't make me
upset
I know how I used to act, that, I didn't forget
And I know that a helping hand can be ignored
But she's not doing this due to being bored

So I offer support as best I can
I feed the hope she will understand
So that her path is better than mine
No emotional drowning, no staying inside

At the end of the day, I thread carefully
Cause I was delicate, and I think she's like me
I fear that just because our pains are alike
I will always feel like trying to catch a train by
bike

I spend a couple of extra minutes praying she'll
be okay
And I cry myself to sleep, imagining what I'd
have done to have someone else say
All the pretty things that I now know are
fundamental
When I felt like my whole existence was just
experimental

But this cycle makes me better and keeps her
here
And though I had it rough, I didn't disappear
Even though no one told me all these things
I found them out, in between flings.

love as a passive verb

My other friends got back with their exes, but I
won't.
Because my heart is still too torn apart to take
itself for dead
Instead of feeling difficult, it'll settle for being
fine
And we will look like friends, but we'll tear at
the seams

This arrangement is perfect because I know what
I want
And when I get upset, I stop. Because he doesn't
owe me an explanation
My anxiety takes that as enough, and I can
afford to be blunt
And he hasn't asked for space or all my
dedication

But love is enraged at us for turning it into
passive.
Such love like ours was never a thing of the
masses
We put it in a secondary plane
Remembering to love, just not to date

So by saying that my status is complicated
By telling him now isn't a time that great
I try to face it and untangle fate
But neither of us is ready to pay the price for
being separated.

a musician's pain

The saddest instrumentals known to man play in
the back of my mind
I love repeated lyrics because I, too, feel like I'm
trying to convince myself over and over
Sometimes, the piano gets loud, or the drums
drown it out
And in that mess of sounds, I can picture a
hangover

I feel perfectly understood but still
underestimated
And my goals make no sense outside my mind
My closure always feels belated
And I'm always looking but hoping not to find

I never try anything that I might like
Because I'm already unstable alone
So I come back with the best stories and
pictures
But I never find quite the place to call home

And they tell me that I speak to their souls
But I know they don't have a mind like mine
No pictures, barely sounds, but thoughts all the
time

The only ones who care to stay call themselves
ghouls

My therapist once told me that I made things
harder for myself
She said that not all my thoughts are wise,
though valid
I never know what's anxiety, feels like a lack of
self
She also tells me to process things, not just close
the lid.

stage fright

I used to be afraid of big crowds.
One time, when I was very little
My favorite singer was late to one of her shows
And I went up there and sang, knowing the
lyrics.

I don't quite know if it's a memory or a cry for
help.
But, anyhow, I forgot everything about my stage
fright
Why did my years bring back the fear of what
others felt?
Did my light get duller when it used to shine
bright?

So in 9th grade, I signed up for a poetry contest
And when I read the poem in front of my whole
school
Suddenly I didn't care for being cool
My words were true, and no one knew the rest

My biggest supporter is also my worst enemy
I know that's a fact since I'm both of them
And I'd give everything to be just a friend of me
But settle for opposing sides until then

So now I'm a stage-fright-full, somehow free,
puzzling masterpiece
I feel like my life has been a series of "eve"s
I cry, scream, and beg for peace
Fighting against other's pet peeves.

outer space dreams

When I think about my future, I picture it in
space
A station, nowhere close to here, learning human
development
My hair would quickly become gray, my heart
would risk atrophy
but I feel deep down that said dream is for me.

I don't know much, however, and I'm constantly
scared
And I fear that if I fail, it will seem as if I never
cared.
But my heart beats for a place much outside this
earth,
And I believe, now, it may have been written at
birth

Canned food and a view to die for
A routine and science as a vital activity
I won't be afraid anymore
I have such an ability

My God knows more about this than I do
By Him, I can hope to see it through
So I study with the hopes of a worthy degree
And I keep going, holding on to what I'll see.

the view from outside

He tells me they broke up with an undertone of
tears
She says sometimes love "just doesn't work"
and
I see it as a personification of all my fears
He tells me that we're not right as I reach the
deep end

A teacher asks me if the sea is hot or cold today
He laughs, "With the two of you, I can never
say"
I barely laugh as I respond, it's only a half-truth
But I also know that the switch-up is a part of
youth

So I tell them I'm here if they want to talk
We could catch a movie, grab a bite, take a walk
And they thank me but always forget to take me
up on my offer
Like they benefit from keeping their feelings in
a coffer

Extending my support over and over
The leaves will fall and the weather will get
colder

One day, the hole will disappear without
scandal
The burden they will see, they can handle.

over it

I heard somewhere that the wind was changing
I'm not afraid of losing what I've been gladly
gaining
You meant everything; you were the only prize
I left, but I wish I stayed for our demise

You and her should start a club of all the people
I've hurt
Those I loved, swept up, then had to leave
The ones who let me wear their shirt
Until I was insufficient, nothing more to weave

So I learned that I love too strongly and too
deeply I dive
I understood all that bees do for their hive
I'd be the wealthiest woman on this earth to
walk
If I gained for every promise broken, every
"second chance" talk.

Not that I'm over it
I could still wish to throw a fit
When she pretends to look away while staring
into my soul

When she pretends to have mastered all that I
know

I say I'm fine with not appearing the best
I'd pass everything she hasn't thought to test
Competition only exists if there's ground for one
Not in this case, cause I've won

But I waste my breath on useless rants
And I convince them to join my chants
Because being over it doesn't mean I'm free
Maybe over it is something I can't be.

a rented home

My weekends almost make me feel like I'm
back home
But after two or three phone calls, that feeling's
gone
So Brazil stays stuck inside a rectangle
And I'm left looking for an unseen angle

I get all the updates on the parties I missed
I hear everything about those who kissed
Everything that was said, felt, and seen
Those who the people there had been

I, in turn, update them on my situation
As complicated as it is, I find some place for
exaggeration
So they tell me my stories are complex and cruel
I respond, "Unfortunately, they're true"

But my life is the only one I'd ever find worth
living
And day after day, I'm never done giving
Because trying will never stop having worth
And surrendering would be much worse.

recovery?

I burn my tongue not waiting for things to cool
I pretend to know love, but I'm just a fool
I run around and around, but I'm difficult
And I seem to be home to some unknown cult

Belief is the most powerful of weapons
And I appear crazy, but no one else reckons
So my diagnosis only confirms what they
surmised
And no one else believes that I was disguised

I sigh and try to gasp for air,
I slip into sudden despair,
My own voice is sick of hearing the talk:
I know that now I should walk the walk.

So left without any taste buds,
Knowing that I failed love,
Wondering how you chose whom to keep,
Realizing I'm in too deep:

I send in my two-week notice,
I come up with reasons to leave.
They say I was too young to know this
And as I go, finally, I breathe

not "ok"

My breathing is drowned out by a cloud of
worries
And like a good partner, he hurries
But the tenuous line between us no longer exists
I'll just wait until it exits

He tells me that the conversation dawns soon
And I present every downside as my pessimistic
self
But I win the trial with no objections, and I
sense he's giving up the will to try
I write the eulogy for our obituary, hoping it
won't double as mine

So now the depths of his skin are unknown again
And we think, one day, we can be friends
But I feel my desires bow out as they begin to
die
And I barely get out of bed, having only the
strength to cry

He uses okay like an all-knowing word
I screamed inside cause I didn't feel heard
And everything we held as sacred now ends up
lost

And the past was just enough for the cost

So I'll reread the novel of our story
He never annotated, called it a waste of time
So I'll leave with what I know, not having
learned and too hurt to try
He'll avoid anything of me, running from his
own mind

I'll say my heart is torn knowing I cried when it
begun
He'll say it's all fine, hiding the spark that's gone
I hold my breath in my hands and accumulate
tears that shine
And I'll never know if he takes down our shrine.

bittersweet

I feel the tears building in my eyes as we hug for
a picture
She's been growing up so fast I can feel it
I look at them from across the room and fake a
smile
If I really try, I can get rid of it for a while

She tells me that she'll visit as I try to hold it in
I know that soon enough, my turn will begin
And someone else crying doesn't make the pain
go away
I'll just digest the lyrics to "Look After You" by
The Fray

The future is scary, but so is the truth
And I'm sick of wanting prohibited fruits
They know better, yet I still fear their help
So how will I know to be better by myself?

But one year of us was more than I could ever
deserve
And I'll always try to, this love, preserve
So, when I cry, don't wipe away the rest of my
tears
Just smile and thank our golden years

garden gossip

I wake up reading messages that would've
caused me to spiral
There's no claim for belief, but I feel like it's
viral
Then my breathing speeds up like the garden I
planted was being destroyed
All of a sudden, I scram to fill the void

And I find myself hating an idea I'd once been
supportive of
I had told you so many times to call it off
Then why do I panic like the ten-year-old inside
is still making decisions?
Like my bags were packed and I was taking
provisions

So as if coming out of water, in seas not that
deep
After making the walk back and finding it steep
I gather ingredients for the potion that makes
them stay
As I write closing arguments, for when I've
saved the day

Cause what offspring would watch as its garden
is killed?
If it fails in acting, how is it truly skilled?
like poisonous seeds, destroying the roots
I admit defeat and send home my troops

meaning

I feel like a foreigner inside my own head
I sense traces of unknown poison that isn't lead
And everything seen is just in my imagination
The world outside is enough cause for
contemplation

But my simile turns into a metaphor
Suddenly, I don't remember who this was for
Is forgetting freeing regardless of the price?
And for lack of a better word, I just call this nice

My intuition is lying to see a better outcome
I happen to like who I have become
My mistakes were sometimes foolish, but so was
I
I'm used to not hitting the bullseye

So my passport only proves an entrance
And my diary sees those in other forms
I refuse to try to comply with the norms
I am something of significance.

3-day trial

I'm offered the opportunity to "wreck a home"
People think they know how it feels to be gone
But their attention is nothing but a desperate cry
And I won't, not out of a need to pry

He tells me I made a mistake, and he was the
right choice
I hear a sudden disappearance of my own voice
They don't know what they're signing up for
No, don't they dare walk through the door

He brings back fears that I buried deep
I fear they bring back the promises I never keep
So the downfall of my empire means nothing to
history
Historians don't think it to be a worthy mystery

So I'll laugh at other bids
Lie whenever I speak to little kids
I'll tell her it's too soon
And I'll vent to the moon

Because what I feel is gone but not post-mortem
I think that the wound is still not visible to them
But it lives far into my lively essence
I'm not a "free-trial" presence

an extension of me

A part of me grows older today
It's been on its own for a while now
And I don't mean to bring about a frown
But she's never been prey

Her fresh-cut hair twirling into a frame
Her lips shining due to lip balm
Her laugh, like she's unaware of the game
And her eyes, always calm

She'll complain that I'm far
I'll joke, "You want me to hijack a car?"
Because such things far apart don't mean any
less
And I think of her when I feel like a mess

5 years a bond strong as it gets
Though hard times, I can say I have no regrets
I know she has my back even when I fall down
And I will never make her clown

it struck a nerve

A belief I didn't even know I had sparks up in
my chest
I argue with my own beginning, restraining from
my best
To lie about something so easy to explain
To feel like my whole identity is in vain

Liking both doesn't mean I'm indecisive
It doesn't mean I was born wrong
But she throws salt in the wound
Adding insult to injury

I feel absorbed by my vices
I feel like throwing away our song
We fight like old gladiators and
We collude in front of the jury

So I step back into the shadows that I believe to
be safe
I fight this undying, unexplainable haze
I feel like making predestined mistakes
A poorly thought-out collection of hot takes

confusion.

There's nothing inherently wrong with you
wanting to be with me
I saw no red flags when you were trying to win
me
But suddenly it's him again
Suddenly I'm just a friend

Call it not the right time
But the conversations between the two of you
happen like ours never do
No such thing as a wasted rhyme
I'll start saying what I think; no further ado

You made me believe there was actually
something
I wanted to make it happen, even though I
wasn't sure
We'll never get a chance to hear our melodies
sing
And what now is tainted used to be so pure

A desire so relevant and so uncertain
Half a lie, even farther from the truth
You claim I want you in front of them
You'd kiss me if we were in a booth

So we'll sit like strangers, divided by a silent
barrier
Like scientists researching a contagious disease
with an unknown carrier
You'll rise like the sun, I'll wait for the morning
We'll both avoid the topic, silent mourning.

unheard melody

I stare at my half-black screen
making sure I can still be seen
I stop to breathe for a second more
at the same time that I know this, I haven't been
here before

Something delicate, beautiful, and kind
Something that never quite leaves my mind
Don't think I could translate such charming
melody
Don't think you could grasp just how much it
means to me

I wake up each morning stuck in that haze
I'm prisoner of this feeling that never fails to
amaze
Prisoner might be somewhat of an exaggeration
I'm more than happy to partake in constant
celebration

But my thoughts all circle through the same
current
Leading into a fear that isn't very apparent
And I never run, I'm way too honored to stay
I vow to focus on appreciating today

long gone

Observe as I go
There's no way to get me to stay
I cut the line you and I used to toe
Maybe we'll be fine someday

Leaving is such an outdated trick
I have learned something from you, after all
I built this courage brick by brick
You had many chances, if you'll recall

You said things swept up by your heart
I did what I had to follow my head
there was no way to do this, "instead"
I couldn't feel farther apart

So my blood will boil, my heart will hurt
I'll believe myself to be the worst
I'll leave us bruised, covered in dirt
You know they say, "you never forget your first"

But art is dramatic, and, frankly, so am I
Not everything that hurts you leads you to die
Other boys and girls might do it for you
Who knows, but hoping is all I can do

pre-show makeup

I wonder how your blonde hair looked while you
twisted the knife
You placed it on my back so carefully
To gain access, you didn't even use a disguise
Just your made-up affection for me

Was it up? Were there curls?
Did you at least spend the time to look
acceptable?
Before doing what is, frankly, despicable
Did you pick out a dress and put on your pearls?

Was it his idea? A judgment lapse?
How many lies will you tell to cover the truth?
Were you having a hard time finding
well-sourced maps?
I'm afraid there's no way to, my thoughts, soothe

So your dreams will now be nightmares
Sleeping on the bed you made
You keep hurting anyone who cares
You'll be left without aid

disappointment

Ever-changing, everlasting
I'm afraid to be too free
All the things that I've been masking
Eventually, catch up to me

A sound mind is what's been lost
After you decided, to me, accost
There's no turning back from here
It's either the truth or the pier

Follow lies all the way down?
A bigger coward than I knew you to be
Running in your self-exile from this town
Never stopping for anybody

Your legs will get sore
The air will get rare
You'll regret every single affair
Crying, mirroring the sky that will pour

Living blameless in your faults
Stepping on toes in every waltz
We'll watch as you take a bow
Only you can save it now

high risk-high reward

I've been watching race car pilots
Speeding, and then speeding more
Our words were said like bullets in riots
You're still the one I adore

Never braking leads to doom
But not stepping on the gas means to lose
Balance is where happiness lies
Even if it takes a number of tries

Protective gear isn't something sure
Letting go is also mature
If you choose to see it through
Someone else might have to lose you

But the higher the gain
The higher the price
We feel alive due to this blinding pain
Ignore every little piece of advice

And we'll draw starting positions
Look at it from the wrong point of view
Risk it all for something new
Before we part ways for our future missions

our song

Tell me it isn't momentary
I know, I feel it too
Nothing about this is ordinary
Can we just stay, see it through?

Your heartbeat is the only tempo I'm following
I'm staying here, gladly wallowing
Nothing's granted, but no way I'm gonna lose
I'll pay the price if I have to choose

Help me pick a chord progression
Create our own special melody
Pour our hearts into the lyrics
Make something precious just for you and me

exiled

They've locked me out of the secret gardens
No more drinking from the fountain of youth
The lack of your presence, the yearning, hardens
I want you to be my truth

But they had fireproof gates made,
They closed them as I cried
Every last wish was denied
And I had to watch as my happiness decayed

I have the key, so it is unfair
To lock me out due to fear of my "affair"
Don't they know that joy lies
When I'm looking into your eyes?

So I'll sneak out and jump the gates
Keeping my steps in close, sneaky eights
When whispering and staying close
No one tells what no one knows

my little teenage brain

My little teenage brain and me
We don't really get along
It gives me value, barely
It doesn't see where I belong

My teenage heart and I
We see things eye to eye
We handhold as we skip through a field of
dreams
And we drown out my inside screams

My little body in itself
It likes creating little feuds
My own life doesn't worry much about my
health
I find comfort in the junkiest foods

My words and those who hear
Seem to be trivial until I think
I'm afraid I'm the only one who cares to make
the link
Will you prove me wrong, dear?